Happy Work-Life

LEARN TO THRIVE 9 TO 5 AND BEYOND

Happy Work-Life
Learn To Thrive 9 To 5 and Beyond

ISBN: 9781983369629

Printed in the United States of America

Book interior design by Jean Boles
https://www.upwork.com/fl/jeanboles

Happy Work-Life

LEARN TO THRIVE 9 TO 5 AND BEYOND

TRACY FOX

ABOUT THE AUTHOR

Tracy Fox is a sought after speaker, best-selling author and NYU certified strategic life coach. Tracy works with clients in three specific areas. One is Personal Coaching, where she counsels men and women who are unhappy, stuck, and don't know what to do about it. Her second area of expertise is in Marriage Coaching, where she consults with couples experiencing conflict or complacency. Finally, she is a relationship expert who teaches strategies to improve and strengthen connections within your home, work and spiritual life.

Tracy has written three other books:

Happy Self – A Three- Step Strategy to Elevate Your Inner Game

* * *

The Having A Heart For God Devotional
365 Days of The One Minute Bible Study

* * *

Happy Marriage Handbook – A 10 Step Solution to Happily Ever After

(This is complimented by an online E-course of the same name.)

* * *

Tracy also sends out a free, weekly, inspirational email entitled, "Happy Life" to thousands of readers. Everything is available at her website:

www.TracyFox.net

Tracy is married to Mark Fox; they live in Darien, CT with their three sons and dog, Finnegan.

To Contact Tracy:
Email: **Tracy@TracyFox.net**

Praise For
Happy Self – A Three-Step Strategy To Elevate Your Inner Game

---

- Loved this book—I keep it on my bedside table. Last thing I read at night. — Kim S
- Exceptional! I will be gifting Happy Self to my entire family. — Margaret M
- In two words – life changing. — Tom A
- This is a wonderful empowering read. We all need a Happy Self and what better time than right now to take care of yourself. Give it a read and you will not be disappointed. — Ridgely B
- Effective strategy that is clearly written and presented in a way that really helps. Was very much worth the purchase. — Steve M
- Super helpful and thought provoking read. Tracy is very clear in outlining the simplest route to clarity. — Kimberly B
- Go beyond the "selfie" and see for yourself how three simple strategies can bring you REAL happiness: from the inside OUT!! — Liz A
- As profound as it is pragmatic. A great resource for a happier life. — Stephen M

- A wonderful read that's simple to incorporate into your life. Making all the difference! — Gwynne T
- I can't recommend this book strongly enough. I think anybody would find smart ideas to enrich their life. It's an easy read with only 16 short chapters but it has the potential for a profound and lasting impact on your life if you take the learning to heart. — Imani J
- A friend recently gave me this wonderful book as a gift. It has provided me such insight on happiness. It will be at the top of my list at Christmas as a gift for friends and family. —Brandi M
- This is an incredible book. It will change your life. We all deserve to live a happy life. Tracy will help you make this come true. I can't wait for my friends to read it. I am buying copies to give out to them. — Meredith S
- Just finished Tracy's book and really enjoyed it - I would recommend this book to anyone who needs a refresher on what's really important in life! — Beatrice C

"This Above All: To Thine Own Self Be True."

— William Shakespeare

Table of Contents

INTRODUCTION

Why Happy Work-Life Matters

LEARN TO THRIVE 9 TO 5 AND BEYOND

There is a well-known quote by Annie Dillard that states, "How you spend your days is, in fact, how you will spend your life." For many of us, a large portion of our waking hours is spent at work. In fact, the average person will spend 90,000 hours at work over their lifetime.

It is basically a guarantee that our work-life will have a huge impact on the quality of our lives as a whole because a job is so much more than a paycheck. Our line of work offers us an avenue to fulfill our vocational purpose, to contribute to an organization bigger than ourselves and to collaborate with lots of different and inspiring people.

Becoming financially secure is good for all of us, but it is not the most important thing for a happy work-life. The key to happiness is much bigger than that. We want to be satisfied with the person we are, the accomplishments we seek and the relationships that are a foundation for a meaningful life. We also might yearn to pursue other hobbies, new adventures or deeper spiritual development. Finally, we need to guard against having our family or health take second place to a one-track pursuit of career achievement.

Yes, it is true that financial security matters because we have bills to pay. However, we also must ask ourselves what is the point of working so hard to afford a backyard pool, a nice car, or a family vacation if we never really get to enjoy any of those things.

More and more young professionals agree with this philosophy. They are seeking jobs with the chance for good work-life balance, even if those jobs typically come with slightly lower pay. They understand the price of burnout which can lead to the loss of ideas, energy, relationships, fun, or the opportunity for a life well lived.

They also have a better handle on the misconception that more money equals more happiness. Studies of different countries find that happiness is actually more prevalent in nations where many individuals live at or just above the subsistence level. Other studies show that increased income provides only a relatively brief period of increased happiness, because once basic needs are met and one splurges on a few extras, more money will actually bring more stress, not more happiness. In fact, a Princeton University study concluded that people are happy with an increase of income up to $75,000 and any other amount higher than that number did not increase levels of life satisfaction.

This philosophy is highlighted in a well-known story credited to Heinrich Boll about the simple life of a fisherman. It goes like this:

One day a fisherman was lying on a beautiful beach, with his fishing pole propped up in the sand and his solitary line cast out into the sparkling blue surf. He was enjoying the warmth of the afternoon sun and the prospect of catching a fish. About that time, a businessman came walking down the beach, trying to relieve some of the stress of his workday. He noticed the fisherman sitting on the beach and decided to find out why this fisherman was fishing instead of working harder to make a living for himself and his family. "You aren't going to catch many fish that way," said the businessman. "You should be working rather than lying on the beach!"

The fisherman looked up at the businessman, smiled and replied, "And what will my reward be?"

"Well, you can get bigger nets and catch more fish!" was the businessman's answer.

"And then what will my reward be?" asked the fisherman, still smiling.

The businessman replied, "You will make money and you'll be able to buy a boat, which will then result in larger catches of fish!"

"And then what will my reward be?" asked the fisherman again.

The businessman was beginning to get a little irritated with the fisherman's questions. "You can buy a bigger boat, and hire some people to work for you!" he said.

"And then what will my reward be?" repeated the fisherman.

The businessman was getting angry. "Don't you understand? You can build up a fleet of fishing boats, sail all over the world, and let all your employees catch fish for you!"

Once again the fisherman asked, "And then what will my reward be?"

The businessman was red with rage and shouted at the fisherman, "Don't you understand that you can become so rich that you will never have to work for your living again! You can spend all the rest of your days sitting on this beach, looking at the sunset. You won't have a care in the world!"

The fisherman, still smiling, looked up and said, "And what do you think I'm doing right now?"

Clearly, the main reason to opt for a job with better work-life balance is simply that if you don't balance work with the rest of your life, you'll miss it. The idea is to have a job you love and a life you love too.

The philosopher Aristotle concluded, "The ultimate end or purpose of all human life is the achievement of personal happiness." The answer to that happiness is what I hope you find in my book, *Happy Work-Life, Learn To Thrive 9 to 5 and Beyond.*

Happy Work-Life outlines how to pro-actively implement strategies that teach you how to thrive in five key areas. Surviving is doing what is necessary to live. Thriving, on the other hand, is the ability to prosper, flourish and grow abundantly. If you desire to live an empowered life where you make the best out of all you have been given, then this is the book for you.

The truth is either you are managing your life or your life is managing you. You can design and create any life you want, so why not build a life with a blueprint of personal peace and happiness as you realize your fullest potential along the way.

Remember to read this book with pen in hand. Each chapter contains question and answer sections with a prompt to "Lock In The Learning." This will encourage you to commit on paper to actions steps toward positive and lasting change.

Enjoy,

Tracy Fox

"Success is not the key to happiness. Happiness is the key to success. If you love what you are doing, you will be successful."

— Albert Schweitzer

CHAPTER 1

Do You, Only Better

LIVE TO YOUR PURPOSE AND PASSION

Have you seen the movie, *Field of Dreams*? Let me summarize. Iowa farmer and long-time baseball fan, Ray, played by Kevin Costner, hears a mysterious voice one night in his cornfield saying, "If you build it, he will come." Ray feels the urge to act, so he decides to build a baseball diamond on his farm, supported by his wife, Annie. Suddenly, the ghosts of great players start emerging from the surrounding cornfields to play baseball, led by "Shoeless" Joe Jackson. But as Ray learns, this field of dreams is about much more than bringing former baseball greats out to play. It is really about creating a life that matters, the life of his dreams!

I am big believer in "if you build it, they will come." In other words If you build your life into the best it can be, one that is true to yourself, true to your ideals, true to your purpose and passion, then all good things will come.

Human beings have been given an amazing gift. We have the power to decide who we want to be and the life we want to create. Philosophers and anthropologists agree that the attributes that make humans unique from all other creatures are our ability to reason morally, make decisions freely and connect spiritually. The concept of free will is bound up with such things as our capacity to choose our own values, the sort of lives we want to live, the kind of people we want to be, and most importantly, the capacity to produce anything we want out of the hand we have been dealt. This is a critical point. We can make a decision today that can positively change the outcome of our tomorrow. So why don't more people tackle their lives with the intention to enjoy the absolute best that life has to offer?

The answer can be found from a nurse in Australia named Bronnie Ware, who spent her career working with dying people in the last 12 weeks of their lives. She routinely asked her patients about "any regrets they had or anything they would do differently." Eventually, she distinctly identified *The Top Five Regrets of the Dying* in a book by the same name. Here they are in descending order:

5. "I wish that I had let myself be happier."

4. "I wish I had stayed in touch with my friends."

3. "I wish I'd had the courage to express my feelings."

2. "I wish I hadn't worked so hard."

1. "I wish I'd had the courage to live a life true to myself, not the life others expected of me."

WOW...let's have a moment on that! Imagine spending your entire life not being true to yourself and then on your deathbed realizing it is too late to do anything about it. We need to pay close attention to these sentiments as it can change the course of our own personal destiny.

To find ultimate happiness in your work-life, the first step is to *do you, only better*. You take all the gifts and deficits you were born with and then you prune and cultivate them over time until you are the best version of yourself you can be. It takes both courage and determination to live to your highest potential life but it is well worth the effort.

TAKE RESPONSIBILITY FOR YOUR OWN HAPPINESS

The first step is to take personal responsibility for your own happiness. You can either live your life as a victim or a victor. Victim personalities have internal dialogues that inform them that life is what happens to them. These people tell themselves that they have no personal power to change their lot in life. They are stuck.

On the other hand, victor personalities conclude that they are fully accountable for the life they live and they consider the notion that all things are truly possible. They understand that to be successful in creating the life of their dreams, they must believe they are capable of making it happen.

Brian Tracy, the best-selling author, explains it this way, "Responsibility is the hallmark of the fully integrated, fully functioning human being. Responsibility goes hand in hand with success, achievement, motivation, happiness and self-actualization. It's the absolute minimum requirement for the accomplishment of everything you could ever really want in life. Accepting that you're completely responsible for yourself and realizing that no one is coming to the rescue is the beginning of peak performance."

We have all been given the privilege of pursuing our personal happiness. In our own Declaration of Independence, we are reminded that the pursuit of happiness is a God-given right. It is written, "We hold these truths to be self-evident, that all men are created equal, that they are endowed by their Creator with certain unalienable Rights, that among these are Life, Liberty and the pursuit of Happiness."

The more accountability we take for the joy in our lives, the more we understand that we have the power to transform our circumstances. As Lou Holtz said, "Life is 10% what happens to you and 90% how you respond to it."

LOCK IN THE LEARNING

If you were responsible for you own happiness, you would have to do WHAT differently.

1____

2____

3____

4____

5____

GO AFTER YOUR DREAMS WITH BRAVERY

We all have aspirations for a prosperous future and that includes a happy work-life. So why do we have so much trouble turning our ideals into reality? I believe it has to do with fear. If you take a close look at the list of the 5 top regrets discussed at the beginning of the chapter, the number one regret had to do with "courage." Those elderly men and women said they wish they had the "courage" to live a life true to themselves. It takes bravery to go after your dreams.

Those who achieve great things are the ones willing to be scared but not scared off. We all fear something. We might be scared of rejection, failure, or not being good enough. We could be frightened of flying, speaking in public or safety concerns. We might be worried about stepping out of our comfort zones or asking for a promotion at work.

However, what separates victors from victims in the game of life is that victors have the dexterity to accept fear as part of the package and to forge ahead anyway. When I coach on fear, I like to give the example of fire fighters. They have chosen a career fraught with uncertainty and danger. When they rush into a burning building there is a level of concern and anxiety over what they will find and the unknown challenges they will face. There are people and pets they need to rescue while they also maneuver building hazards and the safety of their team members. However, firemen conquer their fear with a duty to a higher calling, which is to save a life. The definition of true courage is not that you are never afraid; it is that you are afraid of something and you decide to push forward past it.

Mary Kay Ash, entrepreneur extraordinaire and founder of Mary Kay Cosmetics, is a reminder to all of us about the importance of conquering fear to realize success. She is a woman who started her company with a $5,000 loan one month after her husband, George, died of a heart attack. She said, "When you reach an obstacle, turn it into an opportunity. You have the choice. You can overcome fear and be a winner, or you can allow it to overcome you and be a loser. The choice is yours and yours alone. Refuse to throw in the towel. Go that extra mile that failures refuse to travel. It is far better to be exhausted from success than to be rested from failure."

As an NYU strategic, professional and personal coach, I work with clients regularly who want to conquer their fear. One of my clients, Emily, allowed me to share her story below.

Coaching Story:

I worked with Emily for just under 12 weeks. She contacted me because her business, Financially Fit, was finally getting some press and she has been asked to speak at a local banking conference. Emily was terrified. She did not have any experience speaking in public and had convinced herself she could not go through with the offer. However, she also understood that by saying no to such a great opportunity would be a foolish business move.

I told her that most people believe they only have two choices when they are afraid. One is to stay paralyzed in indecision and the second is to run for cover. However, there is a third option. Be afraid and do it anyway. I told Emily to start small and get comfortable with speaking in general.

Over the next 3 months she took every available chance to speak to a crowd.

(Continued on next page)

> Sometimes it was as simple as leading her book group discussion, another time she volunteered to deliver an opening statement in front of the entire congregation at her church. By the time the banking conference rolled around, Emily was well practiced and confident she could win over her audience.

LOCK IN THE LEARNING

What are your top three dreams?

#1____

____

____

#2____

____

____

#3____

____

____

What fears do you need to conquer to make those dreams come true?

#1____

____

____

#2____

____

____

#3____

____

____

"All our dreams can come true, if we have the courage to pursue them."

— Walt Disney

KNOW YOUR PURPOSE & POTENTIAL

Most highly successful people share one important trait. They align with their purpose and then focus on what they want to achieve. Everything they do and say aim to bring them closer to those goals.

Your life purpose consists of the central motivating desires of your life. It is the reason you get up in the morning. True purpose is about recognizing your own gifts and using them to contribute to the world. You can use those gifts wherever you are including your place of work, out and about with your friends, in intimate relationships with family members, or in service to folks you don't even know.

Purpose can guide life decisions, influence behavior, shape goals, offer a sense of direction, and create meaning. There are several places to discover your life purpose.

Look To Your Heart

Your feelings are your best tool to access your true purpose and passion. Ask yourself what you love to do. Ask yourself what activities inspire you the most. Inquire about what you would do even if there was not a paycheck attached to it. When you lead from your heart, you are naturally more joyful and motivated to explore.

Look To Your Friends and Family

Sometimes other people can observe things about us that we are not capable of noticing. Go get some feedback from family and friends. Ask them what they see you doing with your life and what your ultimate purpose is from their point of view. Be open to their suggestions.

Look To Your Childhood

Try to remember what you did for fun when you were a child. Often the clues to what we are best at came very naturally to us as children. Did you lead, create, draw, teach, or design? Did you play with dolls, cook with the Easy Bake oven, set up Army men or race cars around the house? It sounds silly but often your truest self emerged when you were not even conscious of it. I know from my own childhood, I used to spend hours playing "teacher." I had endless notebooks filled in with crayon notes expressing all the ideas that I wanted to share. Now as an adult, I teach through my courses, coaching, books and speaking. It is what I did then and it is what I do now!

BELIEVE YOU HAVE MORE THAN ONE PURPOSE

You are a complex human being and have many purposes. Just think about the roles you play in your own life. You might be a parent, child, friend, spouse, employee, manager, coach, helper, boss, writer, actor, cook, nurse, driver, speaker, mentor, painter, or dancer. The notion that we have only one purpose limits us from fulfilling our authentic greatness. Be a possibility thinker and try the following life purpose exercise.

LOCK IN THE LEARNING

What did you love to do as a child?

1____

2____

3____

4____

5____

6____

7____

What do you love to do now?

1____

2____

3____

4____

5____

6____

7____

DECIDE WHO YOU WANT TO BE

We are often overly consumed with our "to do" list and less focused on who we want to be. It is always a wonderful exercise to spend some time on the values and character traits we admire and want to improve on in our own self.

David Brooks, a *New York Times* columnist and best-selling author, wrote an intriguing book entitled *The Road To Character*. In it he describes how society's focus on fame, wealth and status eclipses moral virtues and internal struggles. He asserts we have two competing selves.

One self is concerned with resume virtues. As the name implies "resume virtues" are those attributes and achievements that we want to tout in order to build up our own stature.

These are successes and character traits involving things like work ethic, accountability, communication, and leadership. Resume virtues are about accomplishments, performance, and abilities.

The other self is looking for community and connection. This self is concerned with the "eulogy virtues." These are virtues we speak about at funerals when remembering someone's most treasured qualities revealed in empathy, compassion, and love for others.

Mr. Brooks reminds us to be careful not to miss claiming qualities such as kindness, bravery, honesty and integrity amidst the overwhelming forces of a materialistic culture more focused on a job title or the number of vacation homes you own.

One of the qualities I intentionally worked on a couple of years ago was availability. I made a conscious decision to become more accessible to those around me. Now, when I run into someone during the day, instead of giving a quick wave and moving along, I stop and ask that person how they are doing and listen with intent to help. When I go to my son's sporting events, I purposely don't bring my phone so I can focus on the game. When I notice a person who needs help, I find an extra moment to see if I can offer assistance. Deciding to be available has made me a more compassionate person and has had a positive impact on all my relationships.

LOCK IN THE LEARNING

What virtues or values do you want to develop?

1______________________________________

2______________________________________

3______________________________________

4______________________________________

5______________________________________

6______________________________________

7______________________________________

LIVE BY PRINCIPLE

The truth is you can live one of two ways: by preference or by principle. A preference is a feeling of liking or wanting one thing over another. It is a choice based on likes and dislikes or whatever seems best in the moment. Each situation is weighed by emotions, opinions, desires and sometimes even bad judgment. You go one way today and another way tomorrow. Life becomes a "I will see how I feel" scenario. When you live by preference there is no determined course of action. You simply react to whatever is put in front of you. This is a very dangerous way to go through life, as there is no clear direction or destination.

A principle, on the other hand, is a fixed mode of conduct or thinking. When you live by principles then your convictions are set in stone. You know in very certain terms what is acceptable conduct. Core life principles are the fundamental values you decide to commit to day-in and day-out. They help you know right from wrong, and determine if you are on the correct path to fulfilling your life goals. Principles create an unwavering guide to live your best life. A life principle is basically something that drives you to be the best image of yourself every single day. It is an invisible force that defines who you truly are. Life principles have the power to transform you from the inside out, defining how happy, successful and productive you will be.

You can set core principles around any area of your work, home or spiritual life. Some of my clients have set the following principles:

- At three o'clock every day, I put away whatever I am doing, and I am fully focused on my kids when they walk through the door.
- I will only speak words of gentleness and affirmation to my husband.
- I don't use profanity.
- I start every day in gratitude.
- I give 10% of my income to my church.
- I never walk by a homeless person without saying hello and offering them a ride to a shelter.
- I work a full day at my job, and I don't skimp on hours or effort.

LOCK IN THE LEARNING

Name two principles you will live by going forward.

#1____

____

____

#2____

____

____

FINALLY, CREATE A PERSONAL MISSION STATEMENT

You might think of a mission statement as summarizing the purpose of a company and its reason for existing. In much the same way, a personal mission statement is a declaration of who you want to be, what you stand for, and what you want to contribute to the world.

Creating a personal mission statement gives you a way to identify your values, commit to your goals, and put yourself on a path toward whole-heartedness. It is an internal process that comes from the core of who you are. It is a concrete way to put your purpose into words and express as briefly as possible your deepest aspirations. We should all rigorously think through what we want to accomplish in both our professional and personal lives as a spouse, partner, parent, employee, and community member. If you go back over the last couple of pages and look at your answers regarding what you want to do and who you want to be, your personal philosophy should emerge easily. A lot of insight can be taken from the personal mission statements of top executives.

Take a look at these from successful CEO's as they just might serve as inspiration for you:

Richard Branson, Virgin Group – *"To always have fun in the journey of life and learn from my mistakes."*

Mr. Branson is an English magnate, philanthropist and investor. He has founded more than 400 companies, including Virgin Airways. He is a role model for all of us who want to enjoy our lives and also be successful in business too. He is clear in his mission statement that he places a premium on having fun while mistakes are considered a yield sign to attempt something different the next time around. It is such a refreshing viewpoint to let failure be your guide.

Amanda Steinberg, Daily Worth - *"To use my gifts of intelligence, charisma, and serial optimism to cultivate the self-worth and net-worth of women around the world."*

Ms. Steinberg launched Daily Worth in 2009 to help women build wealth. Since then, she's grown her site to more than 1 million subscribers. Steinberg's mission is to help women overcome the guilt, shame, doubts and stigma they face when trying to make money or build wealth. She empowers women to live by design.

Oprah Winfrey – *"To be a teacher. And to be known for inspiring my students to be more than they thought they could be."*

In an issue of *O* magazine, Winfrey recalls watching her grandmother churn butter and wash clothes in a cast-iron pot in the yard. She decided that her life would be more than hanging clothes on a line. She eventually realized she wanted to be a teacher, but never imagined it would be on TV, radio, or her own network and magazine.

It is not just top-level executives that need to integrate all aspects of life with a dynamic personal mission statement. Here are some examples of clients I worked with over the years. Maybe one of these will also inspire you:

1. "To be an outstanding dad and provide for my family."

2. "To be a mentor to the young future leaders of the world."

3. "To be an advocate for those less fortunate who do not have the money or power for justice."

Consider these suggestions as you write your own mission statement:

Keep it short. You want this to be something you can sum up in a single sentence. Remember, this is about focusing your life on what matters most.

Don't forget to include others. Yes, this is a *personal* mission statement, but it should be just as much about the people you want to impact as it is about yourself.

It should change and evolve as you change and evolve. As you grow and continue learning, your mission might evolve. That's natural. As long as you're staying true to the mission you want to accomplish, you can't go wrong.

There are many benefits to creating a mission statement:

- **It defines who you are and where you are going:** Writing your mission statement forces you to dig deep and really think about what matters most to you. It is like having a navigation system that will take you to where you want to go.

- **Gives you perspective on what matters most:** We all may hope to achieve a variety of things, but a personal mission statement can help you put those things in perspective and decide which are most important. This exercise will jump-start your journey to success and happiness.

- **Builds confidence:** Having a mission statement can help you feel more confident, because clarity equals confidence. The more you know where you want to go, the more you can acquire the means to get there.

- **Creates focus and accountability:** Many successful people write their mission statements down and look at them every morning before they start their day. It enables them to stay on track and make progress one step at a time toward their goals.

LOCK IN THE LEARNING

Write your personal mission statement below:

____

____

____

____

____

____

____

____

When you have the courage to stand out and define who you are in a world that is always challenging you to fit in, you will surprisingly find the happiness and peace you seek. It is all about doing you, only better!

"Outstanding people have one thing in common: An absolute sense of mission."

— Zig Ziglar

NOTES

CHAPTER 2

Miracle of Time Management

WORK SMARTER, NOT HARDER, SO YOU HAVE TIME TO ENJOY YOUR LIFE

The essential ingredient to a happy work-life is to work smarter, not harder, so you can spend time on those things that matter the most to you. This is relevant whether you are running a corporation, a small business, or a family. The best path to getting things done efficiently is to become a master of time management.

No matter how you slice it, there are only 24 hours in a day and we are all challenged with how to use our time well. When you don't have control of your time, it's easy to end up feeling rushed and overwhelmed. On any given day, we are all tasked with multiple different projects of varying lengths and difficulties. If you are in an executive role, it might be running a meeting with your team or writing a summary analysis at work. If you are a stay-at-home parent, it could be taking your child to school, buying groceries, and cleaning the house, all while getting to the gym at the end of the day. If you are an entrepreneur, it could be handling all the roles required to keep your own business afloat, from creating spreadsheets to writing a newsletter or attending networking events for your line of work.

Most of us are familiar with bad time management. Consequences of this include missed deadlines, being late, disappointing others and living with endless stress and anxiety. However, the result of good time management is a calmer and more accomplished you. It will allow you to keep effective "to-do" lists, prioritize everything that is expected of you and also seamlessly handle both work and personal tasks.

Now the expression *'time management'* suggests that you are operating as the manager of your most precious asset—time. The importance of time management comes down to how much it impacts your personal and professional life. Time management is organizing your day so that you find the best use for every moment, including additional time to do the things you enjoy and cherish.

TIME MANAGEMENT TIPS THAT ACTUALLY WORK

There are thousands of time management tips and productivity gadgets, but in my experience, the most effective and practical approaches are simple. Here are eight strategies that work:

1. Think and Speak About Time Differently
2. Set Smart Goals on Paper
3. Chunk Tasks Goals and Stick to the Schedule
4. Estimate Time Correctly
5. Keep A Punch List With You At All Times
6. Eliminate Procrastination and Distraction
7. Delegate Your Weaknesses; Play To Your Strengths
8. Progress, Not Perfection

#1 Think and speak about time differently

We have all heard the following statements and have probably all uttered them at one point too.

"I am so busy."

"I have no time."

"Do you have any idea how busy I am?"

"Where did all the time go?"

"I would love to do that but I am busy that day."

"There just isn't any time."

"I can't get to everything because I am so busy."

"I am so stressed out and way too busy."

Henry David Thoreau, the American essayist and naturalist, wrote something very profound about being busy. He said, "It is not enough to be busy, so are the ants. The question is what are we busy about?" And that is the question we need to consider carefully. What are we busy about?

We live our lives enslaved by the concept that we don't have enough time. We act as if some other force has taken over our ability to get things done, and we blame time as the thief that has stolen our productivity. However, the truth is we have more personal power in this area than we tell ourselves. This idea of time poverty is a myth. The first step is learning time management skills that alter our perception of time as well as how we distribute it.

Change How You Define Time

A good place to start is to stop telling anyone else who will listen how busy you are or that there isn't enough time to get everything done. You need to be disciplined about the words you use regarding your perceived lack of time because your convictions can quickly become self-fulfilling prophecies. The truth is we have plenty of time. There are 168 hours in the week. 40 of those are dedicated to work, 56 should be allotted to sleep and that still leaves 72 hours for everything else. 72 hours each week is a lot of extra time.

You can also replace the statement, "I don't have time" with "it is not a priority." The reason to do this is to get you out of the habit of putting everything under the "I don't have time" category. Instead of talking about your life in terms of how busy you are, speak about it in terms of priorities. You might tell your friend, "I can't make lunch, because I am just too busy" but you would never say, "I can't make lunch as it is not a priority." Because you care for your friend, of course, you will now make lunch a priority. The new proclamation helps you get crystal clear about preferences and commitments that are truly important to you.

Review Time Spent

Many people keep a log of their money expenditures when they are planning for responsible budgeting. They write down everything they spend and then figure out where their funds were actually channeled. Other people keep a food diary when trying to lose weight. They analyze where they are getting into trouble with over-consumption or bad choices. In the same way, keeping a time log is also highly effective for finding out exactly how your time is being spent.

Simply write down the days of the week across the top of a page and then write down the hours vertically in a left-hand column. Then fill in each hour of the day of the week. After seven days, evaluate where you actually invested your time. You will see which activities are benefitting your life and which activities are wasted undertakings. Once you have a handle on your schedule you can make appropriate changes that will benefit your life.

Coaching Story

I had a client named Joe who ran his own graphic design firm. He was struggling with anxiety over having too much work and being busy all the time.

I had him keep a time log for one week, and he was shocked by what he found. This was a guy who by his own admission was always complaining about being "busy," and his wife was equally furious that he could not get home for dinner by 6:00 pm each evening. However, when we looked over his time log, he was actually spending over 3 hours watching television and an additional 2 hours cruising social media daily. That is 35 hours a week on screen time. Now we all love a good television show and we want to check in with business colleagues, friends and family on Facebook and other platforms; however, we don't need 35 hours a week to do it. Keeping a time log was a wake-up call to a very busy entrepreneur who really believed he had no free time at all. Joe made some serious changes to his schedule and now finds time to get more done at work and enjoy family dinner too!

Write Out Your Perfect Work Day Schedule

Finally, another exercise you can use to get control over your time is to think about your perfect day. Write out your fantasy schedule and then attempt to stick to it. You will be surprised how easy it is to do this if you are intentional with your time. Simply write it out and make it happen.

It might look something like this:

6:00 am – Wake Up
6:30 – Get Dressed, Have Coffee& Enjoy My Kids
7:00 – Delicious Breakfast
8:00 – In the car, favorite podcast playing, no traffic
9:00 – Arrive in a great mood, meet and greet my co-workers
10-12 – Meetings
12-1 – Power walk and a light lunch
1-3 – Solo time for unfinished business
3:00 – Break for emails and calling spouse to check in
3:30 – Finish up, write punch list for tomorrow
5:00 – Leave Office

6:00 –	Home in time for Little League Game with my son
7:30 –	Dinner with my family
8:00 –	Kids to bed
9:00 –	Light reading, gratitude list, last minute household chores
10:00 –	Watch favorite show
11:00 –	Lights out because I want 7 hours of sleep

When you create your ideal schedule it gives you a tangible guide to achieve your perfect day. Take back your personal power around time! Think about the items and tasks you would want to ensure make it into your agenda. It might include balancing both work and home obligations, time for exercise, special moments with family and friends, finishing work by a certain time each day and getting a good night's sleep.

LOCK IN THE LEARNING

What does your perfect workday schedule need to include?

____

____

____

____

____

____

____

____

____

#2 Set SMART goals on paper

If you write down your goals on paper instead of just having them in your mind, you are more likely to achieve them. Goal setting is not a new concept, but writing goals down is the step that ensures your success.

The magic of written goal setting is that it enables you to make a plan with deliberation and commitment. The actual act of getting goals on paper, not only sharpens thinking about what you may want to achieve, but it also gives a clear destination point.

Just like a GPS, having an end goal sets in motion a series of steps on how to get there. One of the common characteristics of successful people who manage good work-life balance is that they are intensely goal-oriented. They think through on paper where it is that they want to go in life, and they create a clear plan to get there. Their roadmap to success is the list of goals that they have written down.

Greek shipping magnate Aristotle Onassis said, "Always carry a notebook. Write everything down. That is a million dollar lesson they don't teach you in business school!" Ultra-productive people free their minds by writing everything down as the thoughts come to them.

Top-level athletes, business-people and achievers in all fields use written goal setting. There is not a more glaring example of this than Tony Robbins, the motivation guru. Here is a guy who barely graduated from high school and yet he has catapulted himself to international success due his late night infomercials, his captivating audiotapes, and his international bestselling books and sold-out seminars.

Robbins completely changed his life by simply getting clear about what he wanted, writing it down, and then putting it into action. Fortune 500 companies, professional sports teams, and governments alike, now hire Mr. Robbins to inspire their teams. Moreover, he owns nine companies, runs numerous charitable foundations, has written 6 best-selling books and was recently honored as one of the ten "Outstanding People of the World."

Having goals is the fundamental key to success. Goals let us create our future in advance of it actually happening. Setting goals helps us grow and expand, pushing ourselves to transform in ways that, just maybe, we never imagined.

Many times people set goals, but they never quite achieve them. One common reason is that their goals aren't compelling or inspiring. You're much more likely to put time and energy into something that excites you. Think of a goal as a dream with a deadline.

1. Identify your goals: What do you want? Something almost magical happens when you take generalized desires and start defining them more precisely through goal setting.

2. Write down your goals and concrete plans to achieve them: There is a mythical story about the 1953 Harvard Business School graduating class that highlights the importance of written goals. Each student was asked if they had goals for their future and if they wrote them down. Prior to graduation, it was determined that:

- 84% of the entire class had set no goals at all
- 13% of the class had set written goals but had no concrete plans
- 3% of the class had both written goals and concrete plans

When they went back to survey the same graduates 10 years later, it was discovered that the 13% of the class that had set written goals but had not created plans, were making twice as much money as the 84% of the class that had set no goals at all.

However, the 3% of the class that had both written goals and a concrete plan to achieve them were making ten times as much as the rest of the 97% of the class. This 3% has also used SMART goals to accomplish objectives in every area of their life.

SMART is an acronym giving criteria to guide in the setting of goals.

Specific

- Well defined to anyone that has a basic knowledge of the project

Measurable

- Have a way to measure if you have, in fact, achieved your goal

Attainable

- Know if the goal is reasonable and how far away completion is

Realistic

- Within the availability of resources, knowledge and time

Timely

- Enough time to achieve the goal

It is the difference between saying I want to lose weight and I want to lose 10 pounds in 30 days by sticking to a strict diet of 1500 calories a day and walking a mile each afternoon.

LOCK IN THE LEARNING

Goal #1: Write Your Goal Here in SMART form

____

____

____

____

____

____

____

____

Goal #2: Write Your Goal Here in SMART form

____

____

____

____

____

____

____

____

#3 Chunk Down Goals & Stick To The Schedule

Once you have your goals in working order then you must chunk them down into manageable tasks. Often when a project is seemingly gargantuan, it can be daunting to complete. However, the best antidote to anxiety is action, so you need to proceed by dividing the larger project into manageable components that you can act on. The operative term here is manageable and there are many different ways to do this. Some people use "Post-It Notes" while others prefer a bullet point list. Do what is right for you. As I say in coaching, "No one can climb Mount Everest in a week but you can get to base camp." By simply doing the next right thing you will eventually realize all of your objectives.

Using a calendar is the most fundamental step to managing your daily activities. Often if something is not scheduled on your calendar it most likely won't happen. I use a big wall calendar and put all my activities on it with a color code so I can refer to both my professional and personal obligations daily. Because all of these items are on my calendar, they actually get done! Most folks use systems that are connected to their computers and cell phones so they can access their schedule no matter where they are in world. Use your smartphone as your personal assistant to set reminders and ring alarms to help you stay on track.

#4 Estimate Time Correctly

Estimating time correctly is a tough task for many people but it is one of the most essential management skills for a happy work-life. Usually people vastly underestimate the time needed to implement projects. They forget to take into account unexpected events, unscheduled work or the full complexity of a job. The problem arises when they review a task and think it is going to take one-half hour when in reality it takes an hour. If a task takes longer than you think and you have not given yourself enough time to complete it, then this can lead to stress, overwhelm, lateness and disappointment.

To estimate time correctly you must do several things:

1) Start at the end and work backwards. The best way to look at time is to work backwards from your intended target. If you have to be at a meeting at 10:00 am then that means you need to be ready to leave at 9:45 am, which means you need to have all your papers pulled together by 9:30 am, which means you need to be in your office by 9:00 am. If you can make it a habit to calculate backwards instead of forward you will never be late to another appointment or finish a job with things left undone.

2) Plan to be early. When you plan to be on time, you'll either be on time or late. You will rarely, if ever, be early. However, if you target to be early, you'll most likely be on time. So as an example, if you need to be at the airport by 3:00 pm, tell yourself you must be there by 2:30 pm. For your deadlines, submit them earlier than required. This way you put in a shock absorber for unforeseen challenges and road bumps along the way. If you happen to be early, everyone will think you are a super star. Either way, it is a winning scenario.

3) Whatever time you have allotted for a task, add half more. So if you have allotted an hour to finish a project give yourself 90 minutes. If you get it done on time use the extra one-half hour for something else, such as review, and if you end up using all 90 minutes then you estimated correctly.

4) Have a clock where you can see it. Sometimes we are so engrossed in our work that we lose track of time. Having a clock in front of you will keep you aware of how much time is passing. Or use your smartphone to set a timer. If you have an important meeting to attend, set that alarm 15 minutes before you need to leave.

5) Stop when you said you would. The #1 reason why things run over time is because people don't commit to a hard stop. Don't be afraid to interrupt a meeting or end a discussion in a timely manner.

6) Leave buffer time in-between. Leave 10 minutes in between each appointment or task. This helps you wrap up the previous obligation, take a moment for yourself and then start off to the next one. This simple idea will remove all unnecessary stress from your day and allow you to gain control of your time flow.

LOCK IN THE LEARNING

Where do you have the most trouble with estimating time correctly and what will you do about it?

____

____

____

____

____

____

____

#5 Keep A Punch List With You At All Times

Disorder and chaos tend to increase as your day goes on and more demands are put on your time. The best way to get more done in a shorter amount of time is to keep a daily punch list.

Plan your day on paper before it unfolds in reality. Do it in the morning and list all the items that must be accomplished. Once you have your list, identify the three most important things that must get done and number them. The best way to prioritize this is to ask yourself if your day was interrupted due to an unforeseen meeting what on the list would have to get done no matter what. Number them 1, 2 and 3, then challenge yourself to do those three, most important, things first. This way you will end up having a productive day, even if everything doesn't go to plan. Known as the Pareto Principle, in most cases, 80 percent of results come from only 20 percent of activities. Ultra-productive people know which activities drive the greatest results. Focus on those and get more done.

Once tasks are done, check them off and reward yourself for a job well done. It might be a great cup of coffee or a phone call home. This simple strategy allows you to focus on what you did accomplish versus what is still left on your punch list.

Marcus Lemonis, star of CNBC's *The Profit,* makes 'knockout lists' on personalized note cards. He explains it this way, "I get up in the morning and I'll make a list of the five things I want to get done that day, and without exception, I have to get those five things done. If I end up getting some things in addition to that done, great, but I always have my knockout list." Mr. Lemonis keeps these little cards in the closet of his basement. They're long, narrow cards, with his name on top and when he is done with them at the end of the day, he likes to make paper airplanes out of them. It is a really cool way to have goals take flight.

LOCK IN THE LEARNING

Name 10 items for your punch list and circle the three that must get done

1____

____

2____

____

3____

____

4____

____

5____

____

6____

____

7____

____

8____

____

9____

____

10____

____

#6 Eliminate Procrastination and Distraction

Procrastination is often confused with laziness, but they are, in fact, very different. Laziness suggests apathy whereas procrastination is a choice to do something else instead of the task at hand. Procrastination involves ignoring an important and maybe unpleasant activity in favor of something more enjoyable.

To rid your day of procrastination you first need to rid yourself of catastrophic thinking. One of the biggest reasons people procrastinate is because they make a bigger deal out of something in their minds than it is in reality. It might be your perception about how tough, how boring, or how painful something will be. I do this with exercise. It is so much easier in the morning to sit at home with a donut and a warm cup of coffee. I can convince myself that working out is hard, boring, will take forever and might not even have the intended results.

If you want to stop procrastinating you need to change how you think about challenging tasks. Alter your internal dialog from "I need to do this" or "I must do this," which suggests agony, to "I want to do this" or "I choose to do this," which propose that you are in control and have chosen joy in this endeavor. Envision how great the results will be when you get your task done.

Then use these ideas to get going:

- Focus on the doing and not the avoiding.

- Get out a timer and set it for just 10 minutes because small action is still action. Then count backwards so you are in a race against yourself. A little healthy competition makes it fun.
- Find an accountability partner who can check in on your progress.
- Put a reward in place if you complete your mission.

Distractions

Of the country's approximately 100 million full-time employees, 80 percent say they aren't engaged at work and thus they tend to do the bare minimum. Not surprisingly, being a distracted worker can lead to absenteeism, loss of productivity, negative customer service and even internal theft.

The sad fact is that when workers are disengaged, they admit to wasting valuable time spending at least 3 hours a day on non-work items. Tempting activities include surfing the Internet, personal on-line shopping, answering emails, texting, playing video games and office gossip.

It is important not to give into daily boredom and distractions. Here are some simple strategies:

- **Eliminate your time wasters:** Figure out what takes time away from your work. Facebook? Twitter? Email checking? Chatting with co-workers? Set some rules about your distractions at work by only giving yourself set time for personal use.

- **Work at your peak**: Successful people know when they are at their peak. Some people have tons of energy in the morning, while others enjoy working late into the night. Become self-aware of when you feel the most focused, energized, and engaged. Structure your work schedule within that time window.

- **Choose a Positive Outlet:** Try doing something positive when you need a distraction. A few moments to breathe, a quick walk around your place of work, or checking in with a loved one for a few moments of inspiration will lift your spirits and get you back on track.

LOCK IN THE LEARNING

What are your biggest time wasters and what new habit will you enforce to deal with them?

____

____

____

____

____

____

____

____

____

#7 Delegate Your Weakness, Play To Your Strengths

Whether you are a project manager, an entrepreneur, or just someone who needs to get a lot done, delegation can be your best friend. It helps you to maximize your productivity and lighten your load.

If there are duties that can be accomplished by someone else, consider delegating. I would never consider doing my own tax return every year because I know a well-educated accountant would do a much better job than I could. It is smart to delegate those things you are not skilled at or don't have time for. Then you will have additional time for those areas that play to your strengths.

Now there are plenty of reasons why people choose not to delegate. Some people are perfectionists who feel it is easier to do everything themselves; others believe that they won't get credit for a job well done if they hand it off to someone else.

I find that most people will not delegate simply because they do not know how to do it effectively. Delegating tasks is a skill that, like any skill, can be learned and improved over time.

Put these three delegation strategies into practice and notice how your efficiency increases:

1) **Instruct with words and actions**

   After you tell someone what to do, then show them exactly how to do it. It is the defining difference between getting something done half-heartedly and getting something done to completion and satisfaction. Do not instruct with words only, such as "go file these papers"; instead, show a person the filing system you use and how each file should be placed either alphabetically or numerically. These kinds of details enable people to behave their way to success.

2) Trust and verify

Trust someone else to do the job well but then don't forget to verify that they did. You can allow them to do their job without standing over their shoulder, but later check back and have them show you the completed task.

3) Use feedback to close the loop

Review how the project went and then brainstorm ideas on exactly how you and the person you delegated it to can do it better next time. Maybe you need to improve your communication or they need to improve their understanding of the project. Either way, decide to create a win-win scenario for both of you.

Remember, ultra-productive people don't ask, "How can I do this task?" Instead, they ask, "How can this task get done?"

LOCK IN THE LEARNING

What are a few tasks or projects you are willing to delegate and to whom?

____

____

____

____

____

____

____

#8 Progress, NOT Perfection

"Progress, not perfection" is a great motto not just at work but for your personal life too. Why? Because searching for perfection will destroy your ability to appreciate your accomplishments. People who expect perfection often have a core belief that one's value is connected to how well something is done. They believe self-worth comes from production and achievement in every aspect of their life. This can cause harm in many areas, including worry about making mistakes, letting others down, or not measuring up to their own impossibly high standards.

Moreover, when people focus on perfection they tend to be harsh critics of others as well. High standards can ravage important relationships.

Perfectionism isn't sustainable. The path to success is rarely a straight line. Finishing anything takes flexibility to change course and adapt to new circumstances. Focus on progress, day in and day out, and you can make it much easier and enjoyable to reach your goals.

LOCK IN THE LEARNING

In what areas are you a perfectionist? How will you value progress over perfection going forward?

____

____

____

____

____

____

Summary:

Knowing how to manage your time means that you'll be able to accomplish more in shorter periods of time with less effort. When you learn to take control of your time, it will make your life more fulfilling. At work it leads to an energized and motivated workday while at home it leads to free time to enjoy your personal pursuits and family life.

Moreover, great time management will boost your confidence. Since you are more relaxed and in charge, you are given opportunities to take the lead and gain the respect of others around you. You will also make decisions more easily. There will be ample time to consider options and make choices that most benefits your work and home life.

Most importantly, with good time management you will delete stress from your life. You will no longer be "under the gun" to deal with competing activities. Instead, you will operate from flow, where you seamlessly move from one circumstance to the next.

This means you will engage in the things you love and cherish more often. Extra time is a wonderful thing!

"The key is in not spending time, but in investing it."

— Stephen R. Covey

NOTES

CHAPTER 3

Delight Your Audience

A GREAT LIFE IS ABOUT GREAT RELATIONSHIPS

Maya Angelou, an American author and poet laureate, famously said, "I've learned that people will forget what you said, they will forget what you did, but they will never forget how you made them feel."

We all have an audience. It might be our spouse, our children, our co-workers, our customers, our boss, or simply the person sitting next to you today. How are you impacting them by your very presence and how do they feel after an encounter with you?

It is an important question to consider. Nothing is more significant for a happy work-life than our relationships. We want healthy, mutually satisfying connections built on respect, trust, compatibility and collaboration. It is the people in our lives over anything else that create the foundation of joy at work and fulfillment in families. It is up to each of us to become our own "relationship expert."

Relationships at work

We know that in a work environment bosses play key roles in determining a worker's happiness factor. Each year more than half of employees responding to an annual job-satisfaction survey admit they don't leave companies they leave bosses. Having a fair, sympathetic manager who makes employees feel valued is a more crucial element than the qualities of their company as a whole. In all work-related surveys, getting along with co-workers came in as a close second to what is most important to work culture. The top three concerns for employees at work were honesty, fairness, and trust.

Relationships at home

Family identities may vary around the world but they are all basic to the foundational social structure of life. They are a place that, hopefully, provides us with health, wellbeing and love. Family life and social connections can bring us great joy or immense emotional pain, so we need to tend to the relationships that mean the most to us. When Mother Teresa accepted her Nobel Peace Prize, she profoundly proclaimed to the listening audience, "If you really want to bring happiness to the whole world, go home and love your family."

There are three areas to pay super close attention to when dealing with relationships:

1. **Our Appearance**. Did you know that first impressions have long-term consequences? Upon first meeting you, a person will judge you 87% on appearance, 8% on gestures, and 5% on the words you speak. It takes meeting you 20 more times face-to-face to change that person's original idea of you. Ask yourself how you are showing up. Do you smile? Have you brushed your hair or worn a nice outfit? Do you have good posture? How is your handshake? Dress and act the part you want to be.

2. **Our Words**. The skill of using the right words is a potent force. Words have the power to build up or tear down, to encourage or destroy, to inspire greatness or to kill a dream. Learn to encourage from the bottom up

instead of scolding from the top down. A good example would be, "What is wrong with you that you are always late to our meeting?" versus "It seems like you are having trouble getting here on time. Let's look at what might be getting in the way and see if I can help you figure out a different time line."

3. **Our Actions.** Bernard Rimland, an American research psychologist, conducted a study on the principle of the Golden Rule. Each person involved in the study was asked to list ten people he knew best and to label them as happy or not happy. Then they were to go through the list again and label each one as selfish or unselfish. In categorizing the results, Rimland found that all of the people labeled happy were also labeled unselfish. If we want to pursue true lasting happiness, then being a giving person should be a top concern.

LOCK IN THE LEARNING

In each area, what could you improve on and why?

Appearance

____

____

____

____

Words

____

____

____

____

Actions

____

____

____

____

Relationships Are Built On Two Things: Time and Attention

Here are some things you can do differently to boost all your relationships. There are basically four types of relationships that shape our life. They are work colleagues, close friends, romantic partners and family. However, the success of any of these relationships depends on how often we invest in them.

Become a Good Listener

Everyone has the basic desire to be heard and understood. Unfortunately, few of us are taught how to be good listeners. Most people are too busy thinking of what they want to say next to really hear what the other person is communicating. Make a conscious effort to hear what the other person is saying and have the conversation naturally flow from there. People will more naturally bond with you if you demonstrate you are invested in what they are saying.

Show Appreciation

Gallup conducted a worldwide survey asking more than four million employees about the importance of praise and recognition. Gallup concluded that employees who receive regular praise are more productive, engaged, and more likely to stay with their company than those who do not. The survey results also indicated that employees who are praised receive higher loyalty and satisfaction scores from customers.

Praise is the one gift that does not cost any money. People tend to let others know what they have done wrong, but often do not bother to congratulate others for a job well done. Creating positive morale is priceless because job satisfaction for you and others will skyrocket. Show appreciation by finding your colleagues doing things right and telling them how proud you are of their accomplishments.

Add A Personal Touch

A personal touch is any effort that includes a contribution that causes someone to feel uniquely valued. Remembering people's names is the first step to relationship building, and asking them other important aspects of their life continues the process. Invite them to tell you about their family, upcoming events or even their favorite hobby. When you arrive at your office, go out of your way to meet and greet those in your workplace and spend a few moments engaging with co-workers on an intimate level.

Demonstrate Enthusiasm

Do you not just love it when someone is genuinely excited to see you? Think of that person who always makes you feel like a million bucks. They greet you with a huge smile or hug and their generous spirit is palpable. There is nothing better when someone is fully available to ask how you are and spend quality time without rushing off to the next obligation. Everyone is dealing with issues and concerns you may know nothing about, so always proceed with kindness and generosity.

Encourage Team Building Events

Good communication is vital for high performance at work. Team building can help break down barriers in communication. It builds trust, mitigates conflict and increases collaboration. Effective team building means more engaged employees, which is good for company culture. Even if you are not in charge of team building, you can be a team builder in the everyday workplace. Explore the fun nature of group activities that allow other employees to get to know each other in a casual environment. Invite colleagues to meet outside the office or lead a fun lunch and learn.

Be Customer Service Oriented

Whether you actually deal with "customers" or not, it is a powerful strategy to treat everyone as if they are a customer. The best way to be service oriented is simply to ask people how you can help or what specifically you can do to provide something of value for them. It is remarkable the feedback you can receive by simple asking. You might gain new insights into how to improve products, how to create a better experience at work, or how to make more informed business decisions. It also demonstrates that you respect other people's opinions. Studies indicate that dissatisfied customers tell an average of 10 people they know about their bad experience and they won't return again to that place of business.

Coaching Story

Brendan owns an animal hospital in Long Island. He could not get to the bottom of why customers were not returning for their quarterly visits with their cats and dogs. I suggested that Brendan send his sister, Terry, in to his clinic as an "under cover" client to see what a customer experience was really like through the eyes of someone who really wanted to see his business succeed.

(Continued on next page)

This is what Terry discovered. Upon arrival, the receptionist was very friendly but only spoke to Max, the dog, and did not make eye contact with Terry at all. Terry was then taken to an exam room and told the doctor would be right in. There were no magazines or reading material and the metal chair was extremely uncomfortable to sit in for such a long period of time. No one checked back in with Terry to inform her that the doctor was occupied with other patients. Terry sat alone with Max for over 30 minutes. When the vet finally arrived there was no apology for taking such a long time, and when Terry mentioned her frustration, the doctor seemed dismissive. Then when leaving, the woman at the desk was only concerned with payment and did not ask for feedback or a follow-up visit. Even Terry admitted that if this had been a real life scenario, she would not return to this animal hospital with her pet either.

Brendon changed all his company policies around customer service and now asks for regular feedback from clients to make sure every detail is managed properly. Business has doubled since he made the appropriate changes.

LOCK IN THE LEARNING

From the list above, choose two relationship tools that you will employ immediately.

1.____

____

____

____

2.____

____

____

____

VALIDATION & ASSERTIVENESS ARE RELATIONSHIP TOOLS THAT WORK EVERY TIME

Validation

Validation is one way that we communicate our acceptance of others. Validation doesn't mean agreeing or approving. Validation is a way of supporting and strengthening your relationship with someone even if you maintain a different opinion.

Validation is the recognition and acceptance of another person's thoughts, feelings, sensations, and behaviors as understandable. There are many ways to validate another person. Here are just a few that work:

1) **Be Present.** There are so many ways to be present. Examples include sitting with someone when they are having a bad day, concentrating completely on your child describing his/her classroom, or going to a friend's house at midnight to hold a hand when they are in crisis. Being present means giving all your attention to the person you are with.

2) **Accurate Reflection.** Accurate reflection means you summarize what you have heard from someone else in an authentic manner. The intent is to truly understand their experience. It communicates that you care. If you are not comfortable with reflection, you can always reply, "What I hear you saying is" and then repeat back their exact words.

3) **Ask how you can help.** Often people are looking for solutions but they don't want you to fix their problems for them. Instead of just giving your unsolicited advice, ask them if they would like your opinion. Then proceed with gentleness.

There are also many ways we invalidate others. Here are just a few we want to avoid:

1) **Judging:** "You are way too sensitive," and "That is a ridiculous thought," are examples of invalidating other people's experiences. Ridicule is particularly damaging: "Here we go again, complaining about the same old story."

2) **Denying:** "You are not scared, there is nothing to be afraid of" or "How could you want to sleep more, I know you aren't tired." Be careful not to invalidate the other person by saying they don't feel what they are saying they feel.

3) **Minimizing:** "Don't worry about it" and "Why do you always get worked up?" or "There is nothing to be stressed over" are just

three examples of white washing another person's experience.

4) **Nonverbal invalidation:** This includes rolling of the eyes or checking a watch while you are talking with someone. It might also happen when you read texts during dinner or simply show up late to an appointment.

LOCK IN THE LEARNING

Are you validating or invalidating others? How can you improve?

____

____

____

____

____

Assertiveness

Being assertive is a core communication skill that simply means expressing yourself confidently while also respecting the rights and beliefs of others.

Instead of being assertive, many people tend to be either passive or aggressive. Being passive would include not saying what you think or allowing other people to control the conversation. Being aggressive is when you react in anger. Neither of those approaches are effective communication tools.

Assertiveness is based on mutual respect. I like to say, "Speak your truth and do it in love." This demonstrates that you're aware of the rights of others and are willing to express your thoughts while considering other options to work on resolving conflicts. Assertive communication is direct and gives you the best chance of successfully delivering your message.

LOCK IN THE LEARNING

Are you currently a passive, aggressive or assertive communicator? How can you improve?

____

____

____

____

____

____

Create A Stay-In-Touch Campaign

There is also nothing better for maintaining relationships than making the effort to stay in touch with people. It demonstrates you care and it keeps you "in the know" for both business and personal reasons.

There are endless little ways to stay in touch with folks that only take a minute of your time. Call them, send a quick text, write a note, invite them to join you for an event, send them useful information, post on your social media accounts, stop by for a quick chat or simply take a moment to say hello.

A mom in my neighborhood used to always clip the articles on my son's local sports teams and send them to me with a sweet note. It was a simple gesture I have never forgotten.

This is also vital for maintaining intimate relationships during your busy workweek. When I ask couples how often they speak during a typical workday, the answer is almost always "never." It turns out many people believe they are even too busy for a ten minute phone call home. There is absolutely no way to have a rewarding home life if you cannot find the time for the people you love most in the world. As I mentioned earlier, time is our most precious commodity and we must share it wisely.

LOCK IN THE LEARNING

What "stay in touch" campaign can you implement to enhance your relationships?

____

____

____

____

____

____

Conflict Resolution

Conflict resolution is a way for two or more parties to find a peaceful solution to a disagreement among them. The disagreement may be personal, financial, political, or emotional. Below are some strategies to employ during conflict.

- **Negotiate When Possible:** Get in the habit of negotiating conflict. Simply asking the question, "How can we both win?" is a good place to start.
- **Be Curious:** Look at the other person's point of view as a gift. It is a blessing to have another opinion completely different from yours. Be curious and have some fun with where you both see things differently.
- **Remember Conflict Is Not Anger:** Conflict and anger are often associated with one another but they are not the same thing. Conflict involves a difference of opinion while anger is an emotion. It is important to remember that you do not have to get angry when a co-worker or spouse has a contrasting viewpoint.
- **Respond, Don't React:** Finally, learn to respond in situations that upset you and not react. Let's examine the difference. A reaction is typically a quick reply done without much thought. When people react, it often comes

from being defensive with unchecked emotions allowed to run the show.

A response, on the other hand, is more thoughtful. In order to properly respond to a frustrating situation you should leave space between the initial comments and your reply. A response typically contains reasoning and promotes discussion. When we learn to respond and not react, we are in control of both our emotions and the following interactions.

LOCK IN THE LEARNING

What can you do to improve your conflict resolutions skills?

____

____

____

____

____

____

Summary

Our lives are defined by the quality of our relationships, yet few people take the time to hone the skills necessary to become relationship experts. Develop the skills mentioned in this chapter and see how positively it impacts your work and home life. You will find more joy, cooperation and collaboration with co-workers, supervisors, clients, service providers, other professional colleagues, as well as family and friends. However, the most important aspect to great relationships is your ability to exchange meaningful interactions with those who matter most.

> ***"You can make more friends in two months by becoming interested in other people than you can in two years by trying to get other people interested in you."* — Dale Carnegie**

NOTES

CHAPTER 4

The Habits of Happy, Successful People

THEY DO THINGS DIFFERENTLY

Happy, successful people do things differently! Maybe that is why they are happy and successful. These people think differently, act differently and distinguish themselves from unsuccessful people by taking a deliberate path toward their goals.

Researchers from a Harvard Business School studied this phenomenon by interviewing and assessing professionals who had attained great work-life satisfaction. The results of the study found that these people intentionally structured their activities around four major areas:

- **Happiness**: They pursued activities that produced pleasure and satisfaction.
- **Achievement**: They engaged in actions that got tangible results.
- **Significance**: They pursued enterprises that had a positive impact on the people who matter most in their lives.
- **Legacy**: They dedicated time to values and knowledge they could pass on to others.

Let's look at six practices that happy, successful people employ!

#1 A Morning Routine

How you start your day is often how you finish it. When you start the day off right, it allows you to prepare for the challenges ahead. You can avoid dealing with a disorganized household, being late getting out the door, facing endless commuter traffic or standing in line to grab breakfast before you get to the office if you simply set up a morning routine.

Studies show that people who get up earlier and have a morning schedule prosper because they reduce friction in their lives to focus on what they do best. 90% of top CEOs awake before 6:00 am and they stick to a regular morning ritual.

You can do the exact same thing:

- Set an alarm to get up before anyone else in your household and cherish a few moments to yourself.
- Look over your schedule and be prepared mentally for the day ahead.
- Step outside and get some fresh air. Just 10 minutes of fresh air has been found to boost feelings of wellbeing.
- Nurture your body with water, a healthy breakfast, light exercise, or nurture your mind with meditation or a devotional reading.
- Have a regular outfit prepared to wear.
- Go enjoy your day.

Following are a few examples of morning routines from successful business people.

Barbara Corcoran – The Corcoran Group

The famous *Shark Tank* host founded New York City's largest real estate company. Barbara's morning routine involves waking up at 6:00 am, working out for an hour on alternating days and then jogging to the office. She sets apart time to review priorities and then does those things first before she starts her busy day.

Tim Draper – CEO of Draper Associates

Tim Draper is a busy venture capitalist. He wakes up early and plays basketball, showers and eats a three-egg breakfast. His first step is to clear his inbox to remove any bottlenecks for his team and then reflects on what he needs to achieve in the day ahead.

Mark Zuckerberg – Facebook

Mark is known for simplifying his routine by wearing the same uniform every day--gray t-shirt and jeans. He claims it gives him one less decision to make.

Tim Cook – Apple

Tim checks emails first at 5:00 am. He gets over 800 a day. He then exercises at a private gym and goes straight to his office.

Arianna Huffington – Huffington Post

A big part of Arianna's morning routine is about what she doesn't do. She doesn't start the day by looking at her smartphone. Instead, she takes a minute to breathe deeply, be grateful, and set her intentions. She then practices yoga and meditation and then treats herself to a cup of Bulletproof Coffee.

Howard Schultz – Starbucks

He gets up at 4.30 am every morning to walk his three dogs and work out. At 5:45 am he makes coffee for himself and his wife before heading out the door to work.

I must admit I also have a morning routine. I wake up at 6:00 am. Take a quick look at emails to make sure nothing immediate needs my attention. I then make myself a cup of coffee and pair it with a protein bar while I catch up on the morning news. After getting all the kids where they need to be, I sit at my computer to write for an hour. Then I exercise for 20 minutes before I start a full day of coaching or speaking. I find that a morning routine allows me to get an enormous amount of things done before 9:00 am. This enables me to be on top of my game and the rest of the day flows without much interruption.

LOCK IN THE LEARNING

What is going to be your new and improved morning routine?

____

____

____

____

____

____

____

#2 Create A Clean, Upbeat Work Space

Clutter can make you miserable. The typical American home holds 300,000 items. And people's offices also get overwhelmed with papers and other stuff. Cleaning, sorting and moving around all those belongings can make you feel trapped, overwhelmed, and downright unhappy.

However, creating a clean, upbeat workspace will give you mental clarity and lead you to a more productive lifestyle. Here are some tips:

- **Keep It Organized:** One of the best ways you can decrease stress at work is to have a clean workspace. Start small. Throw out anything you don't need, organize papers and rearrange drawers. Put your most used items where they are easily accessible, so that you might increase the flow factor. An uncluttered desk will help you to keep an uncluttered mind.

- **Include Nature:** Living plants, fresh flowers, some sand from your favorite beach, a seashell, or even colorful fish will add a touch of nature and bring the freshness of the outside in. A window is always ideal.

- **Add Personal Items:** Find a photo that makes you smile and bring it to work. Add in your favorite coffee mug, a throw rug, or an illustration of your best affirmation and turn your workspace into a sanctuary. A lot of CEOs have a dartboard, putting greens or framed accolades to remind them that hard work has its payoff.

- **Infuse Color:** Pick out colorful items that are both functional and fun. Vibrant desk accessories and updated, storage solutions with pops of color instantly make your workspace brighter.

LOCK IN THE LEARNING

What is one thing you could do to improve your office space?

____

____

____

____

____

#3 Set and Keep Boundaries

Billionaire Warren Buffet once said, "The difference between successful people and very successful people is that very successful people say 'no' to almost everything." Setting boundaries is the most effective way to protect yourself from daily assaults. Boundaries can be physical and tangible or emotional and intangible. Think about a boundary as a property line that defines where you end and others begin. When you establish healthy boundaries, it is much easier to be an independent person who has a clear sense of their own self-worth and identity. At your place of business boundaries establish what is acceptable or unacceptable workplace behavior.

Ideally, you want to set precedents as early as possible. It is easier to set boundaries from the start than to change them later. Of course, that doesn't mean saying no to everything that comes across your desk or arrives in your inbox, but you should be able to turn down offers that take up too much time, money or risk. And remember, saying "no" now doesn't mean saying "no" forever.

Here are just a few boundaries to be aware of at your place of work:

- Material boundaries apply to your possessions. They determine whether you give or lend things. People in work settings have more of a "what's mine is yours" mentality, so just familiarize yourself with company policy.

- Physical boundaries pertain to your personal space, privacy, and body. There is nothing wrong with a "do not disturb" sign for your door when you need to really focus.

- Mental boundaries apply to your thoughts, values and opinions. No one should ever make you feel devalued at work.

- Emotional boundaries distinguish separating your feelings and responsibility for those feelings from someone else's. Red flags that boundaries are getting crossed are if you feel discomfort, resentment, or guilt. You can think of these feelings as cues to yourself that a boundary issue may need your attention.

A healthy professional boundary is the practical solution to maintaining good work-life balance. It allows you to work at your commitments without over-performing or giving in to unreasonable requests. Boundaries enable you to get clear on your limits and powerfully express them.

LOCK IN THE LEARNING

Which boundary do you need to set and with whom?

____

____

____

____

____

#4 Practice Gratitude

Another habit of extraordinary people is that they are constantly aware of all the reasons they have to be grateful, even while they strive for more. They express their gratitude freely and openly and make it a habit to find good things to concentrate on. Grateful people choose to focus on all of the things that have gone well in their lives. The result is other people want to be in their sphere of positive energy because gratitude is contagious and has an exponential effect on anyone in its grasp.

Ben Smith proves this point exactly. He is an owner of a local car dealership in Miami, Florida that was destroyed by a big storm. Whenever a customer would ask him how business was during that time, he would always answer, "We are doing great and we have so much to be thankful for." People were fascinated by this response as they were used to hearing all the bad luck stories. Customers were so taken with his positive attitude that they went out of their way to get him referrals and he was back in business before anyone on his block.

There is increasing research on the nature of gratitude, its causes, and its potential impact for mental and emotional health. Gratitude shifts your focus from what your life lacks to the abundance that is already available.

How To Be More Grateful:

- Intentionally choose to be thankful.
- Count your blessings.
- Stop focusing on what you don't have.
- Embrace humility.
- Be aware of people in need.

Gratitude is more than just being thankful. It is also about saying thank you. Be quick to offer thanks to those who help you or do a kind deed. It could be your customers, your employees, bosses, co-workers, or the person cleaning your office floors.

LOCK IN THE LEARNING

What is one gratitude practice you will embrace going forward?

____

____

____

____

____

____

#5 Take Breaks

To be happy and successful at work you must break. A "break" is a brief cessation of work, physical exertion, or activity with the intention of getting back to your task within a reasonable amount of time.

- **Movement breaks:** A movement break is essential because light exercise is good for your physical and emotional wellbeing. Constant sitting, whether at your desk, computer, or meetings puts you at higher risk of heart disease, diabetes, depression and anxiety. This is the reason for the uptick in standing desk sales. Getting up from your chair to walk, stretch, do yoga, or whatever activity you prefer can reduce the negative feelings and increase productivity and creativity. It is also a great idea to walk during lunch. Taking a movement break will refresh your mind, body and soul.

- **Meditation Breaks**: With the hectic pace and demands of modern life, many people feel stressed and over-worked. Stress makes us unhappy, impatient and frustrated. It can even affect our health. Try meditation. Meditation is a practice that encourages the mind to slow down so you can be fully present. It is the art of concentrating on one thing as well as the art of being present with experience, emotions

> and thoughts as they occur. Many famous actors, musicians, comedians and business people practice meditation, including Dr. Oz, Madonna, Hugh Jackman, and Ray Dalio, just to name a few.

Meditation at your place of work can be done in less than 10 minutes and will have a huge impact on your feelings of balance and inner peace. Try the following:

Sit quietly, close your eyes and take some deep breaths without worrying about how you're breathing. Take note whether your breath is calm, erratic, shallow, deep, etc. Relax into the breath. Don't worry about how well you're concentrating. You are training the mind to concentrate with no expectations.

Observe the present moment as it is. The aim of mindfulness is not quieting the mind, or attempting to achieve a state of eternal calm. The goal is simple: aiming to pay attention to the present moment.

Don't judge yourself for whatever thoughts surface, just practice recognizing when your mind has wandered off, and gently bring it back to your breath. If you do this regularly, you will achieve a state of calm more quickly each time. The results will accrue. If you are not comfortable trying this on your own, start with an app on your smartphone. Calm and Head Space are two apps I suggest.

Coaching Story

Peter is a principal at a very busy high school. He hired me because he was experiencing burnout at a job he loved. It was negatively affecting his ability to be a role model at the school and, more importantly, a caring husband and father at home. I told him about the importance of breaks in his workday and he was extremely resistant to the idea. "There is no way I can stop during the school day," he complained. "I have a line of students out my door, teachers that need meetings, papers that must be signed and a full schedule each and every day." I asked him if he would be willing try taking breaks for just one week to see if it would change his perspective.

Peter accepted the challenge and we made a plan for a movement break half way through the morning where he would take 10 minutes to just walk around the halls of the school.

Then he also committed to closing his door in the afternoons for another 10 minutes where he closed his eyes and let the stress of the day wash away.

Peter concluded that although he was originally very skeptical about giving up 20 minutes for personal downtime, the benefits have been surprising. He admits he is much more centered and in control which makes him a better leader and educator for the students at his school. Peter is also more relaxed at the end of the day so he can be fully available to the ones he loves at home.

LOCK IN THE LEARNING

How will you take a break during your workday?

____

____

____

____

____

 # 6 Develop A Support Network

Those at the top have learned that success is much harder when you're trying to do it alone. The greater the goals that you're trying to accomplish, the more difficult the obstacles you are going to encounter. American entrepreneur and motivational speaker, Jim Rohn, wisely assessed, "You are the average of the five people you spend the most time with." Take an inventory of which people you are hanging out with and what kind of impact they are having on your decision making and morale.

It is also super important to find people who think differently than you. Always remember that a wide variety of opinions make for a more informed way of thinking about issues. Too much of the same ideas can inhibit growth. You should always strive for diversity and healthy debate. The most outstanding leaders have an eagerness to soak up knowledge and take into account varying perspectives.

Decide to create your own personal "board of directors" for your life or work. Traditionally, a board of directors is a recognized group of people who jointly oversee the activities of an organization. However, for your personal board of directors, they can answer questions about your job, a relationship conundrum or a decision related to health or family. Often, talking through these challenging decisions is the best way to sift through the data and consider all the possible outcomes.

Your personal board of directors exists to act as a sounding board, to advise you and to provide you with feedback on your life decisions, opportunities and challenges. They provide you with unfiltered feedback that you can't necessarily get from friends. Since you are probably not going to pay a fee to your board members, think of other ways to reciprocate.

To get the most out of this advisory group, you want a variety of people of different ages, skills and approaches to decision making. This might include:

- A businessperson in your profession or industry
- A person who has been in your circumstance
- A colleague who is one of your greatest cheerleaders

- A mentor who is ready to critique your decisions because they truly want to see you succeed
- Someone of another generation who can give you perspective
- A connector who can introduce you to others
- A leader in your community

Take your personal board of directors out for lunch every quarter as a group and let them be your sounding board for the new ideas you have about creating a happy, successful you.

LOCK IN THE LEARNING

If you were to create a Board of Directors, who would be on it and why?

My Board of Directors	
Name	**Why did I select them?**

"Happiness is an attitude. We either make ourselves miserable, or happy and strong. The amount of work is the same."

— Carlos Castaneda

NOTES

CHAPTER 5

Unplug, Recharge and Have Fun

INSIST ON SERENITY SO YOU CAN THRIVE AT WORK AND HOME

Growth is good. Everyone wants to be part of a company that is expanding. But if we are not careful there can be a down side of late nights, working on weekends, looming deadlines and stress. Overworking can deplete our physical, emotional, mental and professional welfare.

In Japan many traditional homes are specifically constructed with a wooden footbridge connecting the driveway to the front door of the house. The crossing represents the end of business day and the beginning of personal time. This is an intentional design so that as one walks over the bridge they are deliberately saying goodbye to the workday as they greet their duties at home. This conscious decision prepares the homeowner to be fully present and available to the needs of themselves as well as family/friends once they open their front door. These men and women understand the deep need to nurture all areas of their life so they can thrive. Allow this visual representation of a bridge to be your inspiration as you consider all the ways to unplug, recharge and have fun.

Decompress Upon Arrival

Take a moment to yourself when you arrive home after a busy workday. Set up a new routine. Start with a dedicated space for your most important things, like your wallet and keys. Look for a spot that is easy to access, preferably near your entrance where you'll be able to grab and go the next morning. This way you will never waste another minute looking for your everyday items when you leave for the day.

Then decide what activity will allow you to decompress. Some people ask their spouse for 20 minutes to unwind with a shower and outfit change before re-entry into family life. Others explain to children in advance that they need a few minutes alone after arriving home but promise each child will get undivided attention later in the evening.

Many people go straight into exercise. Even if you feel exhausted after a long workday, just a little workout ensures a palpable increase of energy and stress relief. It is scientifically proven that when you exercise your body releases dopamine, which is a neurotransmitter in the brain responsible for motivation and feelings of wellbeing. Engaging in sports activities wakes you up and clears your minds.

Again, if finding the time to exercise is a challenge, simply change the scope of what you want to commit to. Not everyone has an hour to work out, so do a 20-minute bike ride or 10 minutes of floor exercises instead. Finding a balance between the demands of your job and the requirements of your life is likely to be an ongoing endeavor, but one that is worth it.

LOCK IN THE LEARNING

What will you do daily to decompress when you get home?

____

____

____

____

____

Unplug

We are all highly aware of our obsession with electronics. Here are a few of the statistics:

- 84% of cell phone users claim they could not go a single day without their device.
- 67% of cell phone owners check their phone for messages, alerts, or calls even when they don't notice their phone ringing or vibrating.
- Studies indicate some mobile device owners check their devices every 6.5 minutes.

- 88% of U.S. consumers use mobile devices as a second screen even while watching television.

- Almost half of smartphone owners have slept with their phone next to their bed because they wanted to make sure they didn't miss any calls.

- Traditional TV viewing eats up over six days (144 hours, 54 minutes) worth of time per month.

Making a positive decision to unplug from all electronics for a large portion of your evening will be great for your health and your family life at home. Show your loved ones that they are more important than the screen, and do things the old-fashioned way. Conversations or interactive card games are a good place to start.

Other suggestions could be to remove the TV from the bedrooms. Screen time at bedtime has been shown to influence sleep patterns and lead to less sleep and increased stress. Or ban electronics from the dinner table. Make mealtime an electronics-free zone. Eating with screens on makes you more likely to consume food carelessly and not engage in family dynamics.

LOCK IN THE LEARNING

What will be your new rule about unplugging electronics?

____

____

____

____

Family Meals are a Must

There is no better place for promoting family harmony than the family dinner table. There are an overwhelming number of studies that link family dinners to less high-risk behaviors by kids. This includes anything from problems at school, substance abuse, smoking, binge drinking and even depression and suicidal thoughts. Family dinners promote positive interactions that ultimately contribute to both home life and society at large. Family dinners create a sense of identity, security and love. Researchers say this type of belonging has a more positive effect on kids than even good grades or peer approval.

Of course, the real power of dinners lies in their interpersonal quality of conversation and caring. If family members sit in silence, yell at each other, stare at their cell phones or mock one and other, family dinner won't confer positive benefits. Instead, make this a time to connect through enjoying good food and good fun.

Since work life, school life, and social life can impact your evening schedule, your family meal doesn't need to be dinner. Breakfast or lunch is just as conducive for spending quality time together.

LOCK IN THE LEARNING

What will be your family meal together and how often will you commit to making it happen?

____

____

____

____

____

Go Team Parent

If you are a parent, one of the strategies I suggest for a happy home life I termed, "Go team parent." It means that Mom and Dad present themselves as one unit. You insist that house rules, schedules, and parenting styles unite you instead of divide you. Clearly, both parents want to raise healthy, happy kids, so create a home full of peace and mutual respect. Solid parenting begins when both spouses agree on rules and demonstrate a team approach to how the family will interact.

"Go team parent" means that you and your spouse get super clear on all the tasks necessary to create a happy home and then you work together to get the job done. This is true regardless of who is home and available to parent. Every child is unique and every family deals with issues differently at all the stages and ages of a child's life.

I have coached in many homes and the one thing that creates the most chaos for kids and their parents is not having consistency or clarity around how the family home operates. For the best results both spouses should agree to agree on parenting strategies. Once they are established, never contradict each other in front of your children, do not play "good cop, bad cop" and never have your children get different answers depending on which parent they ask. Remember that kids model a parent's behavior. If you tell your children not to text and drive and then they see you text and drive, they will most definitely text and drive.

Parenting Ideas You Might Try

- Get your kids to buy in. Invite your children to a weekly family meeting. Discuss what works and what all of you can do differently to support each other.
- Mirror back what your children are saying so they feel understood. If a child seems frustrated or angry, you can respond, "What I hear you saying is that you are very upset and angry." This immediately settles them, as they feel acknowledged.
- Speak *with* your kids not *to* your kids. If you want good communication, decide on an activity where you line up shoulder to shoulder before talking with them. This indicates you are on the same side and not in a confrontation. You could take them for a ride in the car, out to a counter for lunch, or for a walk. When kids feel like you are on their

team, they open up much more about their thoughts and concerns.

- Apologize to your kids if you have done something wrong. Have them understand you are also capable of mistakes and able to be sorry for those mistakes.
- Tell your children every day how proud you are of them. Build them up into the people you want them to be. Reward them for effort not results.
- Reading to your children at bedtime is one of the best things you can do to share a moment together.

LOCK IN THE LEARNING

What is one parenting tip you will employ from the list above?

____

____

____

____

HONOR YOUR MARRIAGE

One of the first things to suffer due to an overly stressed work-life is a happy marriage. If you are married, it is critical to put your marriage first. Every statistic on marriage proves that happily married couples do better in every indicator of health and wellbeing.

Let's look at why a happy marriage is good for you and your spouse.

- Married couples enjoy a stronger sense of identity.
- Married couples have richness of social connectivity and belonging.
- Married couples have less stress and live longer.
- In virtually every way that social scientists can measure, married people do better than unmarried or divorced people. They live happier, more intimate and more affluent lives.

A happy marriage is also good for your children. Children from intact married families are:

- More likely to attend college
- Enjoy overall higher levels of happiness
- Less likely to do drugs
- Less likely to become pregnant in teen years
- Less likely to be abused
- Less likely to slip into poverty
- Less likely to go to jail
- Less likely to experience divorce themselves

For better or for worse

Studies on marriage point out that 90% of couples who hit a very serious trouble spot in their marriage, but stayed and did the work to transform their union, are in fact, completely happy again in their married life up to 10 years later. They also report they are pleased they did not go through with divorce as an option.

The truth is that you can create any marriage you want. So why not create the happy marriage of your dreams. In my book, *Happy Marriage Handbook – A 10-Step Solution To Happily Ever After,* there are sections to discuss ideas and brainstorm about every area of married life. You will never regret putting aside special, sacred time for your spouse and family.

Coaching Story:

Beth and Charles reached out to me on the advice of a divorce lawyer. This couple did not really want to get a divorce, but they were not sure there we any other options. Beth complained that Charles was never home because he was really married to his job. Charles complained that Beth did not appreciate the sacrifice he made week-in and week-out to provide for the family. Over the course of their marriage they had become competitors and enemies.

I asked them to stop focusing on all the things that were wrong in their marriage and spend one whole day brainstorming solutions. I invited them to try one of my Happy Marriage exercises. No matter what they disagreed on, I insisted that they tackle the problem with the question, "How can we both win?" This would force them to start thinking and behaving like team players.

(Continued on next page)

They came back to me with this list as a starting place.

- Charles would call Beth every day at 11:00 am for a moment of connection.
- Beth would go to Charles' place of business every Friday for lunch.
- Charles promised to be home by 7:00 pm each evening and put his cell phone away in a basket with no texts or calls until 10:00 pm that night.
- Beth promised to meet and greet Charles at the door with a hug and a warm welcome home.
- Charles agreed to take one night away a month for a romantic rendezvous.
- Beth agreed to go play golf with Charles one day a month with a spirit of fun and playfulness.

I am happy to report Beth and Charles have continued to prioritize each other and their family now flourishes.

LOCK IN THE LEARNING

What is one special activity you could commit to for the sake of a happy marriage?

____

____

____

____

____

Forgive and Forget

The bottom line on forgiveness is that people who forgive are happier, healthier and more empathetic to the world at large. Unforgiving people, on the other hand, tend to be hateful, angry, and hostile, which also makes them anxious, depressed, and neurotic.

Forgiveness is a virtue most of us aspire to. In a nationwide Gallup poll, 94% of respondents said it was important to forgive, 85% said that they would need outside help if they were going to forgive and only 48% said they had even tried to forgive others.

Studies show that people who are not able to forgive completely are still thinking about the ramifications 4-5 years later. That is a lot of time still being angry toward someone. However, forgiveness isn't easy. As C. S. Lewis said, "Everyone says forgiveness is a lovely idea until they have something to forgive themselves."

Here are some tips on how to forgive even when you think you can't:

1) Realize you are first and foremost in need of forgiveness yourself. We have all done things to hurt other people whether we are aware of it or not.

2) Remember, hurt people, *hurt* people. These are the folks that need our love and forgiveness the most.

3) Revisit all the benefits of forgiveness and think about the endless hours you have invested in either obsessing over the infraction or avoiding the person who betrayed you. Decide to proceed differently.

4) Reconcile with humility. Apologize for whatever part you played in the breakdown of your relationship. If the other person

apologizes as well, then accept easily. If the other person cannot see the error of their ways, surrender and let it go.

5) Understand that when you offer unconditional forgiveness, you live a life of kindness and integrity.

SLEEP SUGGESTIONS

We all know that sleep is beneficial to our overall health and happiness. Even without fully grasping what sleep does for us, we know that going without sleep for too long makes us feel terrible and that getting a good night's sleep can make us feel ready to take on the world. While sleep requirements vary slightly from person to person, most adults need between 7 to 9 hours of sleep per night to function at their best.

If you have trouble getting to sleep or staying asleep it may be that you simply cannot turn off your thinking. This is a burden that must be managed. One suggestion that really helps is to listen to a podcast as you drift off. The reason this works so well is that your mind is no longer replaying the details of the day behind you or calculating the worries of tomorrow.

Sleep disturbance can also be related to not producing enough melatonin, which is a hormone in your body that plays a role in sleep. The production and release of melatonin in the brain is connected to time of day, increasing when it's dark and decreasing when it's light. Melatonin production declines with age. You can take a melatonin supplement. I always suggest checking with your doctor to find out what else might be going on and before taking any supplements.

Scientists have gone to great lengths to fully understand sleep's benefits. In studies of humans and other animals, they have discovered that sleep plays a critical role in immune function, metabolism, memory, learning, and other vital functions. Just some of the additional benefits include the following:

Sleep helps reduce stress

If your body doesn't get enough sleep, it can react by producing an elevated level of stress hormones. Deep, regular sleep can help prevent this.

Sleep can lower your blood pressure and keep a healthy heart

Higher blood pressure increases your chances of heart attacks and strokes, but getting plenty of restful sleep encourages a constant state of relaxation that can help reduce blood pressure and generally keep it under control. A regular sleep pattern can help to lower the levels inflammation to your cardiovascular system, which in turn can reduce your chances of a stroke or heart condition.

Sleep leads to a better sex life.

If you are tired all the time, you won't find time for affection or intimacy. Being too tired is the number one reason people note for why their sex lives are non-existent. Bonds of love and connectedness are established in a sexual union with a spouse, so if you want to have a happier sex life, get some sleep.

LOCK IN THE LEARNING

What is one thing you could do to get more sleep?

____

____

____

____

____

SPIRITUAL PRACTICES

We all have the ability to experience inner peace. However, we need to devote time for reflection and solitude. Spiritual practices help us connect to our own selves and also to a divine power. A spiritual practice is the regular performance of activities undertaken for the purpose of cultivating spiritual development.

Having a daily spiritual practice is also important because it:

1. **Takes us inward.** When we are able to separate ourselves from outside stimulation, we finally begin to realize our innermost thoughts. No longer distracted and influenced by what is happening around us, we can know exactly how we feel about certain situations. We can redirect toward self-improvement and progress.

2. **Elevates our minds.** Having a spiritual practice enables us to see beyond ourselves. We are able to view the bigger picture, which then provides clarity and motivates us to set refined goals to a more joyful life.

4. Connects us to a higher power. Spiritual practices take us to a different level of consciousness and help us connect to God.

So whether you want to experience solitude, you are a seeker of ultimate truth, or you practice a particular religion, there are endless ways to explore your spiritual side. Prayer, reading, devotions, yoga, rituals or church attendance, are just a few of the practices to consider.

LOCK IN THE LEARNING

What spiritual practice could you commit to more often?

____

____

____

____

____

____

____

MONEY MATTERS

Several studies over the years indicate that not being confident about your personal finances is a leading indicator of stress and divorce. Research also concludes that arguments about money are longer and usually more intense than other types of family disagreements. Why? People who don't have clarity around their money issues are doomed to defend their position for control. It's not hard to understand why disagreements over money can end so many family relationships. Sharing control of your finances with another person means compromise and trust, which can be difficult even with someone you have known for a long time.

Moreover, men and women traditionally view money differently. It is certainly not true in every situation, but sometimes women tend to view money as a means of security, while men can view it as a source of power. Also, the way someone is raised and family history can play a big role in how one deals with money.

It is a good idea to be familiar with the following financial terms:

1. **Earning:** This is an area to review short and long-term plans for income. How much money do you actually earn and what are you plans for promotion.
2. **Spending:** Here you decide what you want to spend money on. It could be education, travel, leisure, entertainment, or luxury items.
3. **Accounting:** Who keeps track of your overall net worth? Will you have a budget? And how will you divide the financial tasks in your family?
4. **Saving:** This is a place to make decisions about what proportion of your money will go to savings.
5. **Investing:** Look at your risk tolerance and how you want to invest. Do you have plans to start your own business or invest in one? Will you purchase property?
6. **Retirement:** Finally, you'll want to reflect on the plans for your golden years.

LOCK IN THE LEARNING

What type of money management or budgeting do you need to master?

____

____

____

____

____

____

Have Fun – Play Is Serious Business

Establishing space in your schedule for recreation and leisure will help replenish your creativity and problem-solving skills. I tell my clients that play should be serious business because working optimally is all about balance. Unfortunately, most adults have eliminated true play from their lives.

The importance of play for children is well documented. Now researchers are turning their attention to its possible benefits for adults. What they're finding is that play isn't just about fun; it can also be an important means of reducing stress and contributing to overall health. Play provides nourishment for body and soul. For many adults, setting aside playtime is difficult. They struggle with the concept of letting themselves have fun, especially when there are other pressing matters to which they must attend.

Here are some suggestions:

- **Define play correctly.** Play is an activity that is self-directed and where the means are more valued than the ends. In other words, play is about having fun for the sake of fun.

- **Think about play differently.** Try to remind yourself about the importance of play and how it's a positive part of your everyday happiness. Allow yourself a small act of fun every day. It can be something as simple as working on a puzzle or throwing a ball with your pet.

- **You don't have to be "good" at it**. Sometimes people don't play because they think they need to be good at it. I recently bought myself an art set. I go out into my backyard and simply paint the flowers in the garden. While my paintings are not that good, and you will definitely not see them for sale at an art show, the act of painting brings me great joy.

LOCK IN THE LEARNING

What could you do to add more play to your day?

____

____

____

____

____

____

VACATION IS A NECESSITY

Here is a startling statistic: Over 40% of American workers leave paid vacation days unused. I would argue that vacations are not a luxury; rather, they are a necessity. A break from work will provide you with the chance to switch off and recharge for an extended period. It is also a great opportunity to spend quality time with family and friends.

Numerous studies show that vacations increase company productivity and reduce stress. The American Sociological Association compiled a report that suggests that a larger number of vacations lead to a decline in the psychological distress of workers.

The Dalai Lama, when asked what surprised him most about humanity, answered:

"Man. Because he sacrifices his health in order to make money. Then he sacrifices money to recuperate health. And then he is so anxious about the future that he does not enjoy the present; the result being that he does not live in the present or the future; he lives as if he is never going to die, and then dies having never really lived."

To enjoy your vacation, try some of these suggestions:

Don't take the bait

Nearly half of Americans in the Alamo annual vacation survey said they had experienced "vacation shaming" in which colleagues make them feel guilty for taking a vacation and leaving others to pick up the slack. If this happens to you, don't give in to that type of pressure.

Plan well in advance

A well-planned vacation is a vacation that actually happens. Get it on the calendar and inform everyone who will be affected by your time off. Invite co-workers to cover for you so you don't have to "check in" while you are away. Research shows the benefits of planning and looking forward to your vacation are just as important as the vacation itself.

Understand the importance of time off

The reason you work so hard is so you can enjoy your life. Vacationing with your family or loved ones help forge closer bonds. Studies have found women who take vacations with spouses report feeling more satisfied with their marriages. While kids place a higher value on the shared experiences they have on vacations than the material goods they have acquired. Family vacations create more memories than any other activity and that is priceless.

LOCK IN THE LEARNING

What will you do to ensure you take all your vacation time this year?

____

____

____

____

____

Celebrate Your Life

Never forget to appreciate and celebrate the reason you go to work every day. What is your reason? Is it that you love your family and want to provide an amazing life for them? Could it be that you cherish your job as it uses your skills and talents to their fullest potential? Maybe you love your community and your job gives you a unique opportunity to contribute in some meaningful way?

Whatever the reason you go to work, make a decision to design a happy work-life that enables you to thrive, nine to five and beyond. And then celebrate your efforts and your victories daily.

Remember, "If you build it, they will come." Imagine the best version of yourself and work towards being that person every day. Take responsibility for your successes and your failures and learn from role models who have already forged ahead. Live to your purpose and passion. Give generously and be open to the abundance already present. Rest and rejuvenate and be intentional about having fun. Use your time wisely to share the joy you have discovered with all the people that matter most. If you do this, all good things will come.

"There is no passion to be found playing small, in settling for a life that is less than the one you are capable of living."

— Nelson Mandela

NOTES

The Five Secrets To A Happy Work-Life

1

Do You, Only Better

Live To Your Purpose and Passion

2

Miracle of Time Management

Work Smarter, Not Harder, So You Have time To Enjoy Your Life

3

Delight Your Audience

A Great Life Is About Great Relationships

4

The Habits of Happy, Successful People

They Do Things Differently

5

Unplug, Recharge and Have Fun

Insist on Serenity So You Can Thrive At Work and Home

For Personal or Professional Coaching

Tracy works with men and women all over the world. She is available for in person and on the phone consult.

To Find Out More Contact

Tracy@TracyFox.net

www.TracyFox.net

Made in the USA
Middletown, DE
21 July 2018